DAK PRESCOTT

NFL STAR

By Douglas Lynne

Book design by Jake Nordby
Cover design by Jake Nordby

Photographs ©: Nick Wass/AP Images, cover, 1; Greg Trott/AP Images, 4; James D. Smith/AP Images, 6–7, 15; Michael Ainsworth/AP Images, 9; Fred Brooks/Icon Sportswire/AP Images, 10; Don Kelly/AP Images, 12–13; Aaron M. Sprecher/AP Images, 16, 23; Michael Owens/AP Images, 18; Ross D. Franklin/AP Images, 21; Red Line Editorial, 22

Press Box Books, an imprint of Press Room Editions.

Library of Congress Control Number: 2023909339

ISBN
978-1-63494-761-9 (library bound)
978-1-63494-768-8 (paperback)
978-1-63494-781-7 (epub)
978-1-63494-775-6 (hosted ebook)

Distributed by North Star Editions, Inc.
2297 Waters Drive
Mendota Heights, MN 55120
www.northstareditions.com

Printed in the United States of America
102023

ABOUT THE AUTHOR

Douglas Lynne is a freelance writer. He spent many years working in the media, first in newspapers and later for online organizations, covering everything from breaking news to politics to entertainment to sports. He lives in Minneapolis, Minnesota.

TABLE OF CONTENTS

1
THE REAL DEAL

Few people expected Dak Prescott to play during his first year in the National Football League (NFL). The Dallas Cowboys picked the young quarterback 135th overall in the 2016 NFL Draft. However, the team's top backup was injured in training camp. Soon after, starter Tony Romo went down in a preseason game. Suddenly, Prescott was preparing to start the season opener.

After losing his first NFL game, Prescott won his next 11 starts.

Prescott depends on his blockers to give him time to find an open receiver.

Prescott proved that he was ready for the NFL. The rookie led his team to a 5–1 start. But a big test was coming against the Philadelphia Eagles.

The Eagles took a 10-point lead in the fourth quarter. Prescott never gave up. First, his team scored three points on a field goal. A few minutes later, Prescott began a drive from the Dallas 10. He calmly moved the offense up the field. The drive ended when Prescott found receiver Dez Bryant for a 22-yard touchdown. With the game tied 23–23, the teams headed to overtime.

Dallas opened at its own 25. Eleven plays later, the Cowboys reached the Eagles' 5-yard line. Prescott had completed all four of his passes in overtime. Scrambling out of the pocket, he made it five in a row. He spotted tight end Jason Witten wide open in the end zone. Prescott tossed him the ball for a touchdown and the win. It was a dream start to Prescott's NFL career. And he would only get better.

STEPPING ASIDE

Tony Romo was a Pro Bowl quarterback. He had been the Cowboys' starter since 2006. In November 2016, Romo was ready to return from his injury. There was no quarterback controversy in Dallas, though. Prescott was 8–1 at the time. Romo said Prescott deserved to remain the starter.

Prescott threw two touchdown passes and scored a rushing touchdown against the Eagles.

adidas
SEC
MISSISSIPPI
STATE
15
adidas
STATE

2

ONWARD, UPWARD

Dak Prescott was born July 29, 1993. He grew up in Haughton, Louisiana. His family didn't have much money. Dak spent a lot of time playing with his two older brothers. That helped make Dak tough. By high school, he had become a star quarterback.

Teammates were drawn to Dak's hard work and leadership. Dak had plenty of success on the field. Even so, he didn't get

Prescott threw for 9,376 yards and 70 touchdowns at Mississippi State.

Prescott dives for extra yards at the end of a run.

much interest from top colleges. They said his passing wasn't good enough and he was too slow. But Mississippi State University believed in Dak. He soon repaid their faith in him.

The Bulldogs had been a winning team. But they weren't among the top teams in the powerful Southeastern Conference. Behind Prescott, that changed in 2014. After six games, the Bulldogs were 6–0. The undefeated streak included three straight wins over teams ranked in the top 10. Those wins moved the Bulldogs to the No. 1 ranking in the country.

Things eventually came apart for the Bulldogs. After starting 9–0, they finished 10–3. But it was the school's best season in years. And Prescott shattered several school records.

WHAT'S IN A NAME?

Prescott's full name is Rayne Dakota Prescott. As a kid, he didn't like his first name. Instead, his family called him Dak. It was a shortened version of his middle name. His mom got the name Dakota from a 1990s cartoon character called the Dakota Dude.

As a senior in 2015, Prescott led Mississippi State to nine wins. Once again, though, coaches at the next level weren't sure about Prescott. They said his skills needed work.

At the 2016 NFL Draft, the Dallas Cowboys selected him in the fourth round. Almost no one expected to see him on the field for a while.

After getting drafted, Prescott worked with Dallas's coaches to improve as a passer.

KING OF THE COWBOYS

3

Things moved quickly for Dak Prescott in his first NFL season. After beating the Philadelphia Eagles in overtime, his team kept winning. The Cowboys finished 13–3 and won their division. It was only the third time in the team's history that the Cowboys won 13 games. Prescott ended the 2016 season as the NFL's Offensive Rookie of the Year.

Prescott's skills as a runner make him a threat even when his receivers are covered.

Prescott is skilled at making tough throws while running or jumping.

Prescott had proven to be a strong leader and capable passer. Longtime Cowboys quarterback Tony Romo retired before the 2017 season. There was no question that Prescott was now the team's starter.

In the 2018 playoffs, Dallas faced the Seattle Seahawks. With 2 minutes left in the game, Prescott sealed the win with a rushing touchdown. The victory was only the Cowboys' third playoff win in the previous 22 seasons.

The future looked bright in Dallas. However, the Cowboys missed the 2019 playoffs with an 8–8 record. Then Prescott suffered a serious ankle injury during

MAN OF THE YEAR

Prescott's mom, Peggy, died of cancer in 2013. His brother Jace died by suicide in 2020. Prescott set up a group called Faith Fight Finish. It raises money for cancer research, suicide prevention, and other causes. In 2022, Prescott won the NFL's Man of the Year Award. The award is given to one NFL player each year for his outstanding charity work.

the 2020 season. The team still believed in Prescott. Dallas signed him to a new four-year contract that offseason.

Coming back from his injury, Prescott returned to his old form. He led the Cowboys to back-to-back 12-win seasons in 2021 and 2022. Just a few years earlier, no one had known if Prescott would ever be an NFL starter. Now he was one of the league's best.

DAK PRESCOTT
CAREER STATISTICS

- **2016** – 3,667 passing yards, 23 touchdowns
- **2017** – 3,324 passing yards, 22 touchdowns
- **2018** – 3,885 passing yards, 22 touchdowns
- **2019** – 4,902 passing yards, 30 touchdowns
- **2020** – 1,856 passing yards, 9 touchdowns
- **2021** – 4,449 passing yards, 37 touchdowns
- **2022** – 2,860 passing yards, 23 touchdowns

Prescott poses with his 2022 Walter Payton NFL Man of the Year trophy.

TIMELINE MAP

1. **Sulphur, Louisiana: 1993**
   Rayne Dakota Prescott is born on July 29.
2. **Haughton, Louisiana: 2010**
   Prescott leads the Haughton High School Buccaneers to an undefeated regular season as a senior.
3. **Starkville, Mississippi: 2014**
   Prescott's Mississippi State team moves to 6-0 after beating No. 2 Auburn on October 11.
4. **Miami Gardens, Florida: 2014**
   On December 31, Prescott passes for an Orange Bowl-record 453 yards, but the Bulldogs fall 49-34 to Georgia Tech.
5. **Chicago, Illinois: 2016**
   On April 30, the Dallas Cowboys select Prescott with the 135th pick in the NFL Draft.
6. **Dallas, Texas: 2016**
   As a rookie, Prescott leads the Cowboys to a 13-3 record.
7. **Arlington, Texas: 2019**
   On January 5, Prescott's 16-yard touchdown run helps Dallas beat the Seattle Seahawks and secures his first playoff win.
8. **Phoenix, Arizona: 2023**
   In a ceremony on February 9, Prescott wins the Walter Payton NFL Man of the Year Award.

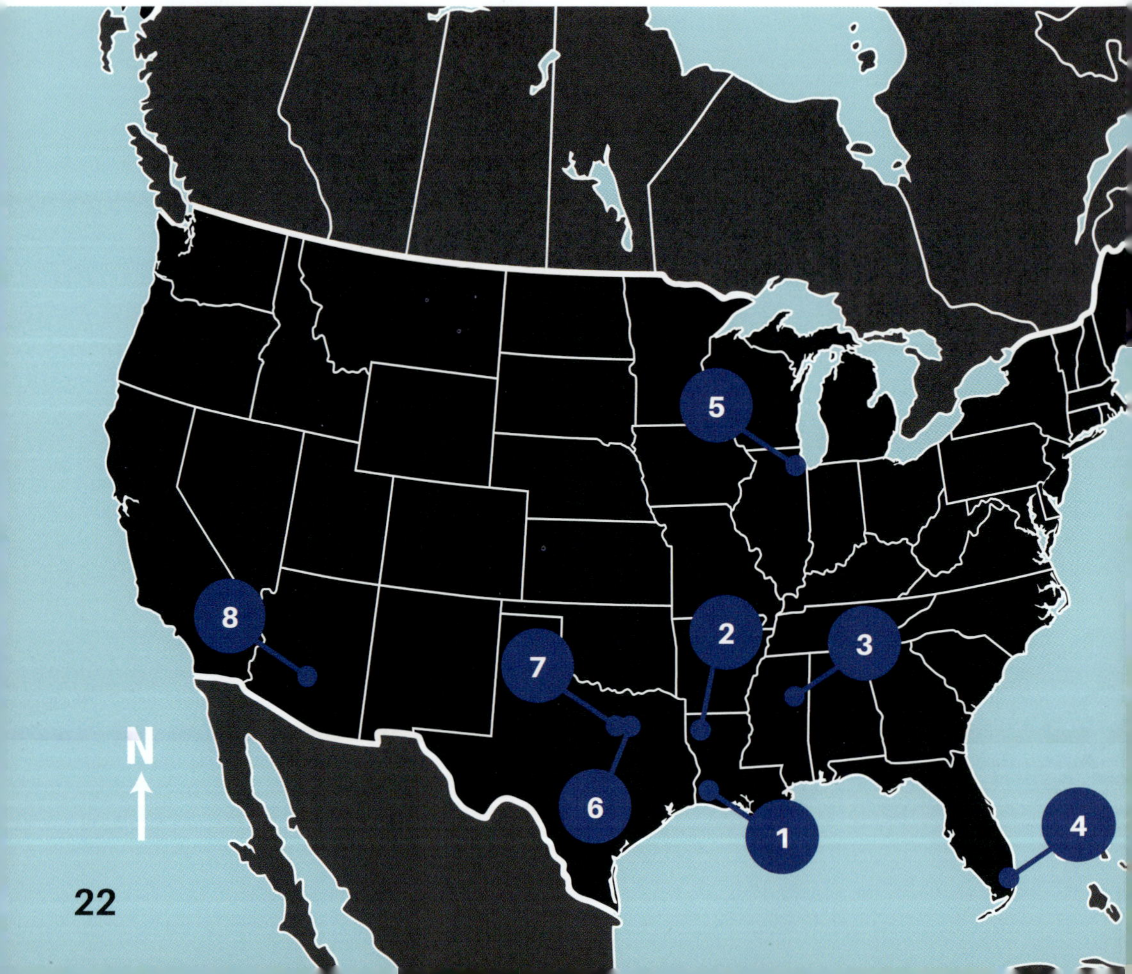

AT-A-GLANCE

DAK PRESCOTT

Birth date: July 29, 1993

Birthplace: Sulphur, Louisiana

Position: Quarterback

Height: 6 feet 2 inches

Weight: 238 pounds

Current team: Dallas Cowboys (2016–)

Past team: Mississippi State Bulldogs (2011–15)

Major awards: First-Team All-SEC (2014, 2015), NFL Offensive Rookie of the Year (2016), Pro Bowl (2016, 2018), Walter Payton NFL Man of the Year (2022)

Accurate through the 2022 season.

MORE INFORMATION

To learn more about Dak Prescott, go to **pressboxbooks.com/AllAccess**.

These links are routinely monitored and updated to provide the most current information available.

GLOSSARY

contract
A written agreement that keeps a player with a team for a certain amount of time.

draft
An event that allows teams to choose new players coming into a league.

drive
A series of plays in which the offense attempts to score by moving the ball downfield.

pocket
An area where the quarterback is protected by the offensive line as he prepares to throw the ball.

preseason game
A practice game that takes place before the regular season begins.

rookie
A first-year player.

scrambling
Avoiding defenders by running with the ball.

INDEX